Kansas

Jill Wheeler

Visit us at
www.abdopublishing.com

Published by ABDO Publishing Company, 8000 West 78th Street, Suite 310, Edina, Minnesota 55439 USA. Copyright ©2010 by Abdo Consulting Group, Inc. International copyrights reserved in all countries. No part of this book may be reproduced in any form without written permission from the publisher. The Checkerboard Library™ is a trademark and logo of ABDO Publishing Company.

Printed in the United States.

Editor: John Hamilton
Graphic Design: Sue Hamilton
Cover Illustration: Neil Klinepier
Cover Photo: iStock Photo

Manufactured with paper containing at least 10% post-consumer waste

Interior Photo Credits: Alamy, AP Images, Baker University, Coleman Company, Corbis, Getty, iStock Photo, Jupiterimages, Kansas Aviation Museum-Wichita, Kansas State Historical Society, Kansas State University, Library of Congress, Mile High Maps, Mountain High Maps, NASA, NOAA, One Mile Up, Peter Arnold, Pizza Hut, Richard Hambrick, Sprint, U.S. Fish & Wildlife-Eric Engbretson, and the University of Kansas.
Statistics: State population statistics taken from 2008 U.S. Census Bureau estimates. City and town population statistics taken from July 1, 2007, U.S. Census Bureau estimates. Land and water area statistics taken from 2000 Census, U.S. Census Bureau.

Library of Congress Cataloging-in-Publication Data

Wheeler, Jill C., 1964-
  Kansas / Jill C. Wheeler.
      p. cm.
  Includes index.
  ISBN 978-1-60453-651-5
  1. Kansas--Juvenile literature. I. Title.

  F681.3.W48 2010
  978.1--dc22
                          2008051043

Table of Contents

The Sunflower State.. 4

Quick Facts 6

Geography 8

Climate and Weather 12

Plants and Animals... 14

History.. 18

Did You Know?.. 24

People 26

Cities 30

Transportation... 34

Natural Resources 36

Industry.. 38

Sports 40

Entertainment... 42

Timeline.. 44

Glossary.. 46

Index.. 48

The Sunflower State

About 90 percent of Kansas is flat farmland. Yet Kansans will tell you there is more to their state than meets the eye. The rest of the state contains rolling hills, stunning rock formations, and marshes.

Kansas plays an important role in growing food for the entire country. The state has a huge underground water supply. It is called the Ogallala Aquifer.

Kansas is well known for producing airplanes. The state's largest manufacturing industry is in aviation.

Kansas has a rich history. Many Kansans were leaders in the anti-slavery movement. They worked hard to end segregation. Many Kansans also served the United States in World War I and World War II.

A state of rich land with beautiful wildflowers, Kansas is known as the Sunflower State.

Quick Facts

KANSAS

Name: Kansas comes from a Native American word that means "people of the south wind."

State Capital: Topeka, population 122,113

Date of Statehood: January 29, 1861 (34th state)

Population: 2,802,134 (33rd-most populous state)

Area (Total Land and Water): 82,277 square miles (213,096 sq km), 15th-largest state

Largest City: Wichita, population 361,420

Nickname: Sunflower State

Motto: *Ad Astra per Aspera* (To the Stars through Difficulties)

State Bird: Western Meadowlark

State Flower: Wild Sunflower

State Tree: Cottonwood

State Song: "Home on the Range"

Highest Point: Mount Sunflower, 4,039 feet (1,231 m)

Lowest Point: Verdigris River, 680 feet (207 m)

Average July Temperature: 78°F (26°C)

Record High Temperature: 121°F (49°C) in Fredonia on July 18, 1936, and near Alton on July 24, 1936

Average January Temperature: 30°F (-1°C)

Record Low Temperature: -40°F (-40°C) in Lebanon on February 13, 1905

Average Annual Precipitation: 27 inches (69 cm)

Number of U.S. Senators: 2

Number of U.S. Representatives: 4

U.S. Postal Service Abbreviation: KS

Geography

Kansas is the 15th-largest state in the United States. It has an area of 82,277 square miles (213,096 sq km). It is the third-windiest state in the country.

Millions of years ago, Kansas was covered in ocean water.

The Sternberg Museum of Hays, Kansas, displays a famous fish-within-a-fish fossil collected in 1952 from western Kansas.

Thanks to all of that water, scientists have discovered many fossils of sea animals in Kansas.

The Ogallala Aquifer is an amazing underground water storage space that is beneath Kansas and other states. It can hold one quadrillion gallons, or 908 cubic miles (3,785 cubic km), of water. That's more water than is held by Lake Huron, one of the Great Lakes.

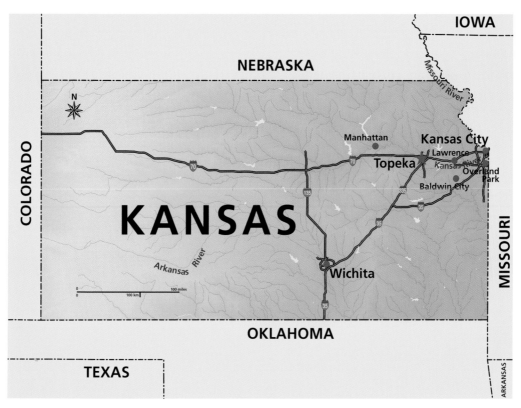

Kansas's total land and water area is 82,277 square miles (213,096 sq km). It is the 15th-largest state. The state capital is Topeka.

People in western Kansas are lucky to have part of the Ogallala Aquifer underneath them. The aquifer is this dry area's main source of water.

Western Kansas is a part of the High Plains. It has very few rivers or trees. It is the highest part of the state.

The Plains Border is in the middle part of Kansas. It contains interesting rock formations, hills, and dunes.

The Southeastern Plains, the Osage Plains, and the Flint Hills are located in the southeastern part of the state. This region features wild tallgrass and bluestem grass. Bluestem grass is good for grazing cattle.

The final region of the state is the Dissected Till Plains. This is a hilly, forested area with many creeks and springs. There are also a lot of valleys here created by glaciers.

Several large rivers run through Kansas. The Kansas River is in the northeast. The Arkansas River is in the south. The Missouri River makes up the northeastern border of Kansas. The Missouri River is surrounded by marshes and wetlands.

A researcher gathers grasses from a Kansas prairie.

Climate and Weather

The eastern third of Kansas has more rainfall, higher humidity, and less sunshine than the rest of the state. The central third of Kansas is at a higher elevation. It has more wind, less rainfall, and less humidity. The western third, or High Plains, is the highest, driest, and sunniest.

Freezing winter winds often blow across Kansas. Sometimes they bring blizzards. Kansas gets an average of 17 inches (43 cm) of snow per year. During the summer, Kansas gets hot winds from Mexico and Texas.

Kansas is famous for tornadoes, just like in *The Wizard of Oz*. An average of 39 tornadoes hit the state each year.

A twister threatens a house near Mulvane, Kansas, in 2004. That year Kansas had a state record of 124 tornadoes.

Plants and Animals

The Flint Hills of eastern Kansas are very rocky and cannot be farmed. The hills are covered in more than 40 different kinds of grasses and many wildflowers. Juniper is the only evergreen tree that is native to Kansas. Forests of elm, hickory, and cottonwood trees run along the banks of the rivers. These forests provide homes for ducks, beavers, woodland birds, badgers, foxes, bobcats, deer, and wild turkeys.

Central Kansas is home to the Cheyenne Bottoms Wildlife Area and the Quivira National Wildlife Refuge. These refuges protect the wetlands. Many birds live there. They include falcons, eagles, whooping cranes, and piping plovers. Also native to central Kansas are blue jays, cardinals, robins, sparrows, owls, and woodpeckers.

A barn owl stands in grass on the Kansas prairie.

Great Egret

Wild Turkey

Peregrine Falcon

Western Kansas is covered by buffalo grass and tumbleweed sage. Other beautiful plants growing there include sunflowers, evening primroses, clovers, columbines, goldenrods, and wild morning glories.

The lakes, streams, and rivers of Kansas include bass, wipers, walleye, crappies, and channel catfish.

Kansas reptiles include collared lizards, skinks, and whiptails. There are about 38 species of snakes in the state, including poisonous copperheads and rattlesnakes.

Channel catfish are one of the most numerous catfish species in North America.

Wildflowers grow on a plain in Cedar Bluff State Park, Kansas.

History

Before European settlers arrived, several Native American tribes lived in the Kansas area. They included the Kansa, Osage, Pawnee, and Wichita tribes. In the 1600s, other tribes moved to the area, including the Arapaho, Cheyenne, Kiowa, Comanche, and others.

Native Americans hunted buffalo on foot. This was very hard and dangerous. This changed after the Spanish explorer Francisco Vásquez de Coronado arrived in the area in the early 1540s. Coronado and his men left behind some of their horses. The Native Americans soon learned to use them to hunt buffalo more effectively.

In 1803, President Thomas Jefferson purchased Kansas and other land west of the Mississippi River from France. This was called the Louisiana Purchase. American pioneers began moving west to settle the new territory.

Spanish explorer Francisco Vásquez de Coronado sees a herd of buffalo.

Kansas also played a key role in the history of slavery in the mid-1800s. Before the Civil War, the United States government asked states to choose whether to be a slave state or a free state. Kansas was at the center of this fight. Before it became a state, people from both sides rushed to Kansas. After many deadly fights, anti-slavery groups finally won. Because of this violence, the state was called "Bleeding Kansas."

Kansas became the 34th state on January 29, 1861. Kansans continued their anti-slavery fight during the Civil War. Some 20,000 Kansans fought in the war, and 3,000 died.

The town of Lawrence, Kansas, was attacked and burned by a pro-slavery group in August 1863.

In the late 1870s, Kansas was considered a leader in equality. In a 10-year period, 26,000 African Americans moved to Kansas. This was called the "Exodus." Many of these people moved to Nicodemus, Kansas. Nicodemus was one of the first towns founded by an African American. Years later, the 1954 Supreme Court case of *Brown vs. Board of Education* began in Kansas. This case eventually decided that separate but equal was not legal. The new law allowed all children, black and white, to go to school together.

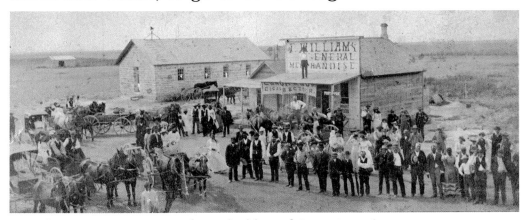

Nicodemus, Kansas, was founded by African Americans.

Many Kansans suffered greatly during the Great Depression of the 1930s. At the same time as the Depression, Kansas

Dust Bowl winds pile up large drifts of soil around buildings near Liberal, Kansas, during the 1930s.

had to deal with a terrible drought. Little rain fell in Kansas from 1931 to 1935. Huge windstorms filled the air with dust. People began calling this period the Dust Bowl. The dust-filled air caused lung diseases. The drought led to many farmers losing their farms and many people going hungry. *The Grapes of Wrath,* a novel by John Steinbeck, takes place during the Dust Bowl. People were very relieved when the rains came again.

A huge dust storm approaches the town of Elkhart, Kansas, in the late 1930s. People suffered greatly during this time of terrible drought. Little rain fell in Kansas from 1931 to 1935.

Did You Know?

- The Coleman Company sells coolers  used to keep drinks and food chilled. The company got its start in Kansas by renting oil lamps to miners.
- Kansas boasts a park built around an old, outdated mining machine. The giant orange machine, named "Big Brutus," is 160 feet (49 m) tall. It is located in West Mineral, Kansas. Visitors can even climb to the top of this huge mining shovel.

Big Brutus gets painted. Workers need a lift to get up to the mining machine's side.

- Motorists in western Kansas may be surprised by Monument Rocks. These huge white rocks appear virtually out of nowhere, after miles of completely flat vistas. These rocks are made out of the chalk that was at the bottom of prehistoric seas. Settlers used them as a landmark.

Monument Rocks

- Visitors to La Crosse, Kansas, can visit the Barbed Wire Museum. Barbed wire was used by settlers to keep cattle from breaking through fences. This unusual museum features the history of barbed wire and its role in the settling of the West.

Barbed Wire

- The town of Codell was hit by tornadoes on May 20 every year for three years—1916, 1917, and 1918.

People

Amelia Earhart (1897-1937) was born in Atchison, Kansas. She was the first woman to fly alone across the Atlantic Ocean. Later, she set the record for the fastest solo flight across the same ocean. It took her 14 hours and 56 minutes. In 1937, she was trying to become the first woman to fly around the world at the equator. Near the end of the trip, she disappeared over the Pacific Ocean. People have searched for her body and her plane, but neither has been found.

Dwight David Eisenhower (1890-1969) was the 34th president of the United States. He was born in Texas, but grew up in Abilene, Kansas. During World War II, Eisenhower was a five-star general who led the Allied forces in Europe against Nazi Germany. Starting in 1953, Eisenhower served as president of the United States for two terms, or eight years. His popular nickname was "Ike."

General Dwight D. Eisenhower stops for lunch by the roadside.

Dwight D. Eisenhower served as president from 1953-1961.

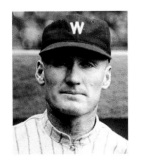

Walter Johnson (1887-1946) was a great baseball pitcher. He was born in Humboldt, Kansas, and spent 21 years in the major leagues. Johnson pitched for the Washington Senators and won 416 games. He holds the record for the second-most games won by a pitcher in major league history. He was also one of the first players in the Baseball Hall of Fame.

Carrie Nation (1846-1911) was a native of Medicine Lodge, Kansas. She gained fame through her campaign against alcohol. Nicknamed "The Woman with the Hatchet," Nation used a hatchet to destroy places where alcohol was being served. Nation's methods often were frightening and violent. However, she inspired others to fight against alcohol.

Lucy Hobbs Taylor (1833-1910) was America's first woman with a degree in dentistry. At first, dental colleges wouldn't accept her. But after working for several years, she was finally accepted to the Ohio College of Dental Surgery. She graduated in 1866. She later moved to Lawrence, Kansas, where she was a successful dentist for many years.

Photographer **Gordon Parks** (1912-2006) was born in Fort Scott, Kansas. He became famous because of the pictures he took of poor people. His photos appeared in an important magazine called *Life*. Later, he became the first African American to direct a Hollywood movie.

Cities

Wichita is the largest city in Kansas. It has a population of 361,420 people. Several

Lightning strikes over downtown Wichita, Kansas.

major aircraft companies are located in Wichita. The city produces more aircraft than any other city in the United States. It is often called the "Air Capital of the World." Wichita is also home to the Exploration Place science museum. Exploration Place features three theaters and a huge park with a playground and mini-golf.

Overland Park is the second-largest city in Kansas. It has a population of 169,403 people. This city is home to a big park with some 300 acres (121 ha) of trees and flowers.

Sprint World Headquarters is in Overland Park.

Kansas City, Kansas. The buildings of Kansas City, Missouri, rise in the background.

Kansas City, Kansas, with a population of 142,320, is located across the Missouri River from another Kansas City.

Kansas City, Missouri, is actually larger than Kansas City, Kansas. Kansas City, Kansas, is the third-largest city in the state. There are many interesting buildings in the city. The Rosedale World War I Memorial Arch is a replica of the Arc de Triomphe in Paris, France.

Gov. Robinson

Topeka is the capital of Kansas and the state's fourth-largest city. It has a population of 122,642. Topeka is a Native American word meaning "a good place to dig potatoes." Topeka was founded by Dr. Charles Robinson, the state's first governor. Some people believe Topeka's limestone capitol building is haunted.

Topeka has other attractions, including an auto-racing facility, a combat air museum, and a zoo.

The capitol building in Topeka, Kansas.

Three other cities in Kansas are notable for their colleges. The University of Kansas is located in **Lawrence**. The University of Kansas is known for

its basketball program. Lawrence also has a several museums. It is the sixth-largest city in Kansas, with a population of 89,852.

Kansas State University is located in **Manhattan**, Kansas. This town is home to 51,707 people. Many of them are college students.

Baldwin City, population 4,202, is home to Baker University, the state's first four-year college. Baker holds a collection of rare Bibles, including a

first edition of *The King James Bible*.

Transportation

Kansans have been building airplanes since the early 1900s. The state's wide-open spaces make flying easy. One of the state's most famous planes was

A 1922 Laird Swallow plane manufactured in Wichita, Kansas.

Jake Moellendick's Laird Swallow. By the 1950s, the state was the center of aircraft manufacturing in the United States.

Kansas also was important to the United States railway system. By 1880, more than 3,000 miles (4,828 km) of track had been laid by 200 different companies. The Atchison, Topeka and Santa Fe Railway was one of the biggest in the nation.

An engineer waves from the window of an Atchison, Topeka and Santa Fe Railway train.

Today, Kansas ranks third in the country in its number of miles of roadway. The state's major highways include interstates 70, 135, 35, and 335. The Kansas Turnpike was one of the first interstate highways to be completed.

Natural Resources

About ninety percent of the land in Kansas is farmland. Kansas is the top wheat producer in the nation. It also is the leader in producing grain sorghum.

Wheat

Kansas farms also grow corn, hay, and soybeans. On average, each Kansas farmer raises enough food every year to feed 129 people. The state is well known for raising beef cattle and hogs. Kansas farmers raised nearly 2 million hogs in 2007.

Kansas is ranked ninth in hog and pig production in the U.S.

Some Kansas farms have been at the center of an argument about farming.

The state is home to many large commercial farms. These farms can raise more animals and grow more crops than most family farms. Some people believe these big farms are hurting smaller family farms.

Kansas is one of the top 10 oil producers in the country. Southwestern Kansas has the largest natural gas field in the country. Kansans also mine helium, coal, limestone, and salt.

An oil drilling operation in western Kansas. Kansas is one of the top 10 oil producers in the country.

Industry

Most people hear the word "Kansas" and think of wheat. However, fewer than 10 percent of Kansans work on farms. The rest live and work in cities. The largest manufacturing industry in Kansas is aviation, or airplanes. In fact, 22 percent of the state's manufacturing jobs are in aviation.

Workers build planes in Wichita, Kansas.

Kansas factories also make food products, printed materials, machinery, and rubber and plastic products. The state also ranks in the top 10 for people working in technology fields, such as communications.

Several famous businesses got their start in Kansas. Pizza Hut was started by two brothers. They began the restaurant with just $600. Pizza Hut now has grown to be a national chain. Sprint Communications also was started in Kansas.

Both Pizza Hut and Sprint Communications got their start in the state of Kansas.

Sports

College basketball is one of many popular sports in Kansas. The University of Kansas and

Kansas State Wildcats fans run onto the field after a 1998 win.

Kansas State University both have talented basketball teams. In 2008, the University of Kansas men's basketball team won the NCAA National Championship.

Other popular teams include the Kansas City Wizards, a soccer team, and the Wichita Thunder, a hockey team.

Football has an interesting history in Kansas. Historically, Kansas State University was known as one of the worst football teams in its conference. Following that, the team had an amazing comeback. From 1993 to 2003, the team won several conference titles and played in 11 straight bowl games.

Kansas is also home to many outdoor activities. Overland Park has 15 miles (24 km) of bike and hiking trails. Kansas also had the first 300-mile (483-km) motorcycle race. In fact, races continue to draw more fans than any other activity. Hunting is popular in Kansas, too. Only two other states have more pheasant and bobwhite quail hunting than Kansas.

Biking is a popular sport in Kansas.

Entertainment

The Kansas Museum of History in Topeka is the center for historical research in Kansas. The museum holds maps, photos, the state archives, and other rare documents. Another museum, located in the town of Hays, is called the Sternberg Museum. It is home to the fossil of a mammoth.

A completely different kind of museum is the Native American Heritage Museum. Located in Highland, Kansas, the museum shows guests how Native Americans once lived. Visitors get to grind corn, make patterns with beads, and play music with a rattle.

Liberal, Kansas, is home to an annual pancake race every February. Racers have to run down the street flipping pancakes as they go. The event takes place on the same day as a similar pancake race in Olney, England.

Runners wearing head scarves and aprons flip pancakes in frying pans in the annual Liberal pancake race.

Most people love to go to the zoo. There is a zoo in Manhattan, Kansas, that might not be as popular. The Kansas State University Insect Zoo is filled with all sorts of bugs. Visitors can pet a tarantula or hold a cockroach—if they really want to.

Cockroach

Timeline

 **1541**—Spanish explorer Francisco Vásquez de Coronado is the first European to travel through Kansas.

 **1682**—French explorer René-Robert Cavelier de La Salle claims the area for France.

 **1803**—Kansas is included in the Louisiana Purchase, making it a part of the U.S.

 **1855-1861**—Kansans fight over whether the state will be a slave state or a free state.

 **1861**—Kansas becomes the 34th state.

1954—The U.S. Supreme Court outlaws segregation in public schools in a case that started in Topeka, Kansas.

1966—The Topeka Tornado strikes on June 8, 1966. Rated an F5, the worst tornado, it injures more than 500 people and kills 16 others.

1980s—Kansas economy suffers because of low oil prices and farm failures.

1990s—Kansas economy improves, businesses expand.

2008—The University of Kansas men's basketball team wins the NCAA National Championship.

Glossary

Aviation—Related to airplanes.

Barbed Wire—A metal fence with pointy metal spikes built into it.

Commercial Farms—Farms which are very large and not family owned.

Dune—A hill made out of sand.

Dust Bowl—In the 1930s, an area of the United States' Great Plains, including the state of Kansas, which was over-farmed and then had little rain for several years. High winds swept across the dry land creating huge dust storms.

Equality—Equal rights for all people regardless of their color, religion, or whether they are male or female.

Equator—Earth's widest part at the center of the planet.

Founded—Created (as in a town).

Glaciers—Large layers of ice that grow and shrink when the climate changes. Glaciers change the land beneath them.

Grain Sorghum—A grass used for cereal.

Great Depression—A time in American history beginning in 1929 and lasting for several years when many businesses failed and millions of people lost their jobs.

Hatchet—A type of ax.

Louisiana Purchase—The purchase by the United States of about 530 million acres (214 million ha) of land from France in 1803.

Mammoth—Extinct relative of the elephant.

Marsh—A type of wetland with lots of tall grass.

Prehistoric—Existing before history was written down.

Segregation—The separation of people based on the color of their skin.

Separate But Equal—A legalized system of segregation.

State Archives—A collection of records about a state's history.

Index

A
Abilene, KS 27
Arapaho (tribe) 18
Arc de Triomphe 31
Arkansas River 11
Atchison, KS 26
Atchison, Topeka and Santa Fe Railway 34
Atlantic Ocean 26

B
Baker University 33
Baldwin City, KS 33
Barbed Wire Museum 25
Baseball Hall of Fame 28
Big Brutus 24
Bleeding Kansas 20
Brown vs. Board of Education 21

C
Cheyenne (tribe) 18
Cheyenne Bottoms Wildlife Area 14
Civil War 20
Codell, KS 25
Coleman Company 24
Comanche (tribe) 18
Coronado, Francisco Vásquez de 18

D
Dissected Till Plains 10
Dust Bowl 22

E
Earhart, Amelia 26
Eisenhower, Dwight David 27
England 43
Europe 27
Exploration Place 30

F
Flint Hills 10, 14
Fort Scott, KS 29
France 18, 31

G
Germany 27
Grapes of Wrath, The 22
Great Depression 22
Great Lakes 8

H
Hays, KS 42
High Plains 10, 12
Highland, KS 42
Hollywood, CA 29
Humboldt, KS 28
Huron, Lake 8

I
Ike (*See* Eisenhower, Dwight David)

J
Jefferson, Thomas 18
Johnson, Walter 28

K
Kansa (tribe) 18
Kansas City, KS 31
Kansas City, MO 31
Kansas City Wizards 40
Kansas Museum of History 42
Kansas River 11
Kansas State University 33, 40
Kansas Turnpike 35
King James Bible, The 33
Kiowa (tribe) 18

L
La Crosse, KS 25
Laird Swallow 34
Lawrence, KS 29, 33
Liberal, KS 43
Life 29
Louisiana Purchase 18

M
Manhattan, KS 33, 43
Medicine Lodge, KS 28
Mexico 12
Mississippi River 18
Missouri River 11, 31
Moellendick, Jake 34
Monument Rocks 25

N
Nation, Carrie 28
Native American Heritage Museum 42
Nazi Germany 27
NCAA 40
Nicodemus, KS 21

O
Ogallala Aquifer 4, 8, 10
Ohio College of Dental Surgery 29
Olney, England 43
Osage (tribe) 18
Osage Plains 10
Overland Park, KS 31, 41

P
Pacific Ocean 26
Paris, France 31
Parks, Gordon 29
Pawnee (tribe) 18

Pizza Hut 39
Plains Border 10

Q
Quivira National Wildlife Refuge 14

R
Robinson, Charles 32
Rosedale World War I Memorial Arch 31

S
Southeastern Plains 10
Sprint Communications 39
Steinbeck, John 22
Sternberg Museum 42
Supreme Court 21

T
Taylor, Lucy Hobbs 29
Texas 12
Topeka, KS 6, 32, 42

U
United States 4, 8, 20, 27, 30, 34
University of Kansas 33, 40

W
Washington Senators 28
West Mineral, KS 24
Wichita, KS 30
Wichita (tribe) 18
Wichita Thunder 40
Wizard of Oz, The 12
World War I 4
World War II 4, 27